T0392316

HE CAN'T COME IN

FATIMA STRAUGHN

ILLUSTRATORS: DEJA MANNS AND FATIMA STRAUGHN

To order additional copies of this book, contact:
Xlibris
1-888-795-4274
www.Xlibris.com
Orders@Xlibris.com

ISBN: Softcover 978-1-7960-6013-3
          EBook   978-1-7960-6012-6

Print information available on the last page

Rev. date: 10/09/2019

HE CAN'T COME IN

LIST OF ALLERGIES

Soy
eggs
milk
nuts
fish
shellfish
shrimp
lobster
crab

Did you know facts ?

Having an epi pen (epinephrine) can help save your life during a allergic reaction.

DEDICATION

To my son Danige, my muse "it's all your fault" to my mom, Thank you for everything. To my dad "thank you for the cape" and to my best friends Ju, Rhi, and Keke Thank you for seeing my magic. And to my cousin who was a very picky eater, this ones for you. - Tee

It's a bright and sunny day in Healthy Town, and Peanut is super excited to start his first day of school at Healthy Town Preschool. Peanut has been talking about making new friends all weekend long.

Because Peanut has a special vegan diet, his mom packs his lunchbox with organic foods. Peanut grabs his backpack and they walk out the door. On the way to school, Peanut tells his mom about all the fun he's going to have with his new friends.

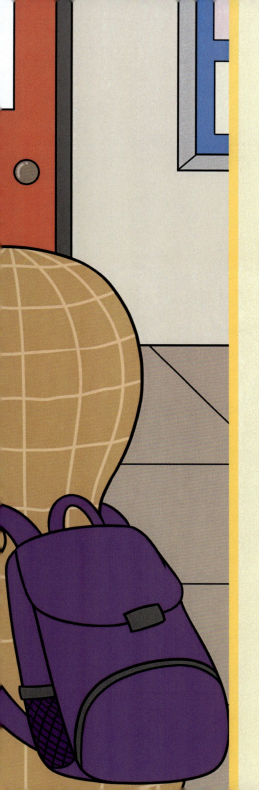

As they enter the school, a few kids stare with wide eyes and point at Peanut, whispering to each other. Curious as to why but still eager to make friends, he smiles and waves at them. Shortly after arriving, Peanut and his mom are called into the principal's office.

Once inside, Peanut and his mom introduce themselves to the principal, Ms. Berry. Peanut notices a picture of an older man on the wall behind Ms. Berry's desk. Ms. Berry realizes that Peanut is fixated on the picture and says…

claude cashew

Elliot Egg

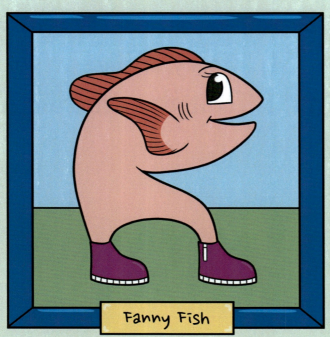

Fanny Fish

Shelly Shrimp

"His name was Claude Cashew. His first day at Healthy Town was certainly one to remember. The first day he walked into his class, all the students became sick. Many broke out in hives, and some were even sent to the hospital. There have been similar cases since Claude, like Elliot Egg, Fanny Fish, and Shelly Shrimp."

With a confused look on his face, Peanut asks Ms. Berry, "Where are those children now?"

"They are in class," Ms. Berry answers. "Would you like to meet your new classmates?"

Peanut jumps out of the chair in excitement. Ms. Berry continues to explain that since the days of Claude Cashew, the school had created a special class for the children considered to be allergies.

Peanut waves goodbye to his mom as she leaves and grabs the principal's hand. Together they head down the hall to his new class. Some students in the hallway stare at Peanut as he walks into the classroom. He remembers the same looks from earlier, but now he understands that those kids are just a bit nervous because they are allergic to him.

Peanut looks around the classroom. It's so bright and colorful. There are books and toys everywhere. When the students spot Peanut hiding behind Ms. Berry, they all run over to greet him.

During lunchtime, the children get to know each other better and talk about how much they can relate to each other. They have many things in common, but are also unique in their own ways. Peanut cannot wait to tell his mom all about his new friends in his special class, and about the fun he had on his very first day of school.

ABOUT THE AUTHOR

Fatima Straughn was born and raised in the South Bronx a talented artist and single mother of a now teenage son who inspired her decision to leave the fashion industry after many years to work along chidlren. A preschool teacher known for her unique personality and teaching style feeding her students wild imagination sharing her love of art with every child she encountered in 2015 she decided to start writing children's books that her son and students will enjoy reading.

ABOUT THE ILLUSTRATOR

Deja Manns is a New York-based illustrator from the Bronx. She recently graduated with a degree in Computer Arts from SUNY Oneonta. Mostly a digital artist, Deja has had a passion for drawing, creating characters, and storytelling since she was a child.

Printed in the United States
By Bookmasters